The More I See Of Men,
The More I Love My Cat

Daisy Hay

Illustrated by Alex Hallatt

summersdale

Summersdale Publishers Ltd
46 West Street
Chichester
West Sussex
PO19 1RP
UK

www.summersdale.com

Printed and bound by Proost, Belgium.
ISBN: 1 84024 421 6

The More I See Of Men,
The More I Love My Cat

Cats sulk quietly in their beds. They do not draw attention to their unhappiness by huffing loudly and banging doors.

4

Cats can be housetrained.

Fat cats can be put on diets. They won't order a meat-feast pizza and cheesy chips when they think you're not looking.

Cats don't answer
back – or at least not in
a language you understand.

Cats don't hijack half
the kitchen utensils for
use in the garage.

Cats understand the
need to spend
time preening.

Cats don't point out
when you have spots.

Cats don't scratch their
nether-regions when
talking to you.

Cats know exactly
when to keep out
of your way.

Cats still love you
on a bad hair day.

Cats only really complain
when they are hungry.

Cats wash regularly.

Cats appear interested when you tell them the same story for the umpteenth time.

Cats don't laugh at you
for singing along
to Kate Bush.

Cats don't expect you to spend
your whole weekend
watching football.

Whiskers are an attractive
feature on a cat.

Treating your cat to
a fancy dinner will only
set you back about 40p.

Cats comfort you
when you are ill.

Cats don't get bored when you're
on the phone talking
to your girlfriends.

Cats don't take all
the bedcovers.

You somehow don't
mind if your cat
has a hairy back.

Cats are never late for dinner.
Never.

Cats don't moan all the way through your favourite weepy that they're missing *Match of the Day*.

Cats don't hog the
ice cream, or make
you feel bad for eating it.

Cats don't get possessive
over the remote control.

Cats don't smoke.

Cats can be neutered if
they wander too much.

Cats don't leave their
dirty socks down the
back of the sofa.

Cats appreciate the
need for frequent
snacks and naps.

Cats are only interested in
your cleavage if it's ample
enough to sleep in.

Cats don't criticise
your driving.

Cats don't leave soiled
underwear on the
bathroom floor.

Cats don't leave
the loo seat up.

Cats don't generate
huge piles of
dirty washing.

Cats don't elbow you
out of bed in their sleep.

Cats don't bring
other loud, obnoxious
cats home after the match.

You never have to try
to impress your
cat's mother.

A cat never misses
the litter tray.

Cats at least pretend
to pay attention to you.

You only feel slightly put
out when a cat rubs up
against your best friend.

When a cat spends
all day sleeping it's
rather endearing.

When a cat goes
to the toilet you don't need
to open all the windows.

You can put your cat
outside when it gets
on your nerves.

Cats don't snore.

A cat can fend for itself (although
they do have trouble with
tin openers).

A cat is always sober, even
after a night out.

Cats are pleased rather than
panicked when you come home
with huge bags of shopping.

A cat is unlikely to have
a violent or obsessive ex-lover.

All you need to do to
keep track of your cat is
put a bell around its neck.

A cat's friend is less
likely to get on your
nerves, and easier
to get rid of.

A cat would never trade you
in for a younger model.

Cats are never derogatory
about your mother.

If a cat jumps onto your knee,
they can be kept happy
with a little cuddle.

There's a slightly better
chance of training a cat.

It isn't overly upsetting if your cat
brings a bird home every
now and then.

You won't outgrow your
relationship with your cat.

Cats never claim they
can fix the video to
prove their manhood.

Cats don't sulk and
whine until you let
them get a new 'toy'.

Cats are always
impeccably smart.

Cats don't go bald,
or fret that they might.

Cats don't get a complex
if they find out you're
older than them.

When a cat comes in
at midnight it doesn't
need carrying to bed.

You are unlikely to
harbour secret longings
for your best friend's cat.

Your cat loves rubbing
against your legs regardless
of how much cellulite you have.

Cats are cute
without trying.

Cats don't develop
beer bellies.

Your cat knows you are the key
to their happiness, rather
than presuming they're
the key to yours.